WS

A Pet's Life

Goldfish

Anita Ganeri

Heinemann
LIBRARY

www.heinemann.co.uk/library
Visit our website to find out more information about **Heinemann Library** books.

To order:
☎ Phone 44 (0) 1865 888066
🖹 Send a fax to 44 (0) 1865 314091
💻 Visit the Heinemann Bookshop at www.heinemann.co.uk/library to browse our catalogue and order online.

First published in Great Britain by Heinemann Library, Halley Court, Jordan Hill, Oxford OX2 8EJ, part of Harcourt Education.
Heinemann is a registered trademark of Harcourt Education Ltd.

Editorial: Jilly Attwood and Claire Throp
Design: Richard Parker and
Tinstar Design Limited (www.tinstar.co.uk)
Picture Research: Rosie Garai
Production: Séverine Ribierre

Originated by Dot Gradations
Printed and bound in China by South China Printing Company

ISBN 0 431 17765 1
07 06 05 04 03
10 9 8 7 6 5 4 3 2 1

British Library Cataloguing in Publication Data
Ganeri, Anita
    Goldfish – (A Pet's Life)
    639.3'7484
A full catalogue record for this book is available from the British Library.

Acknowledgements
The publishers would like to thank the following for permission to reproduce photographs: Alamy **p. 26**; Alamy Images **p. 4**; Corbis **pp. 5** (Robert Pickett), **11** (Michael Keller), **23** (Michael Boys); Dave Bevan **p. 25**; Dave Bradford **p. 27**; DK Images **p. 6**; Getty Images **p. 7** (Photodisc); Haddon Davies **pp. 8, 9, 10, 14, 16, 17, 18, 19, 20, 24**; RSPCA **p. 22**; Tudor Photography **pp. 12, 13, 15, 21**

Cover photograph of reproduced with permission of Photomax.

The publishers would like to thank Pippa Bush of the RSPCA for her assistance in the preparation of this book.

Every effort has been made to contact copyright holders of any material reproduced in this book. Any omissions will be rectified in subsequent printings if notice is given to the publishers.

RSPCA Trading Limited (which pays all its taxable profits to the RSPCA, Registered Charity No. 219099) receives a royalty for every copy of this book sold by Heinemann Library. Details of the royalties payable to RSPCA Trading Limited can be obtained by writing to the Publisher, Heinemann Library, Halley Court, Jordan Hill, Oxford, OX2 8EJ. For the purposes of the Charities Act 1992 no further seller of this book shall be deemed to be a commercial participator with the RSPCA. RSPCA name and logo are trademarks of the RSPCA used by Heinemann Library under licence from RSPCA Trading Ltd.

Contents

Any words appearing in the text in bold, **like this**, are explained in the Glossary.

What is a goldfish?

A goldfish is a type of fish that lives in cold water. People have kept goldfish as pets for hundreds of years.

Goldfish come in different shapes and sizes.

Here you can see the different parts of a goldfish's body and what each part is used for.

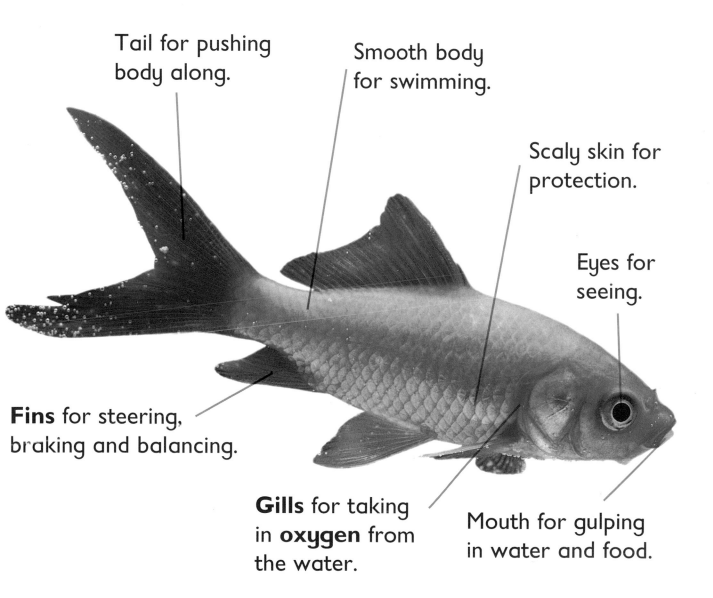

Tail for pushing body along.

Smooth body for swimming.

Scaly skin for protection.

Eyes for seeing.

Fins for steering, braking and balancing.

Gills for taking in **oxygen** from the water.

Mouth for gulping in water and food.

5

Goldfish babies

Goldfish **hatch** from eggs. The female lays thousands of eggs in the water. The eggs are sticky and look like blobs of jelly.

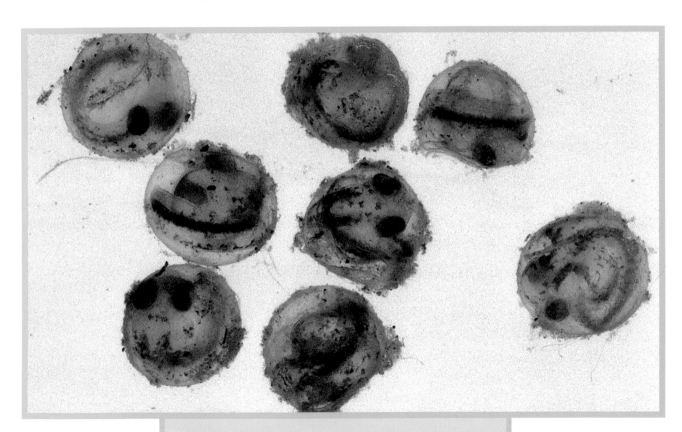

Goldfish eggs are the size of pinheads. They stick to plants.

The baby goldfish are called fry.
It takes the fry about four months to
grow into adult goldfish. Their bodies
are still a dark colour.

A goldfish becomes shiny
orange at about six months old.

Your pet goldfish

Goldfish make great pets and are fun to keep. But you must be a good pet owner and care for them properly.

Your goldfish will depend on you for all of its needs.

If you go away on holiday, make sure that someone looks after your goldfish. Ask a friend or neighbour to call in every day.

Always make sure that your goldfish has the right food and that its tank is clean.

Choosing your goldfish

You can buy your goldfish from a good pet shop, a garden centre or from a fish-keeper's club.

Before you buy any fish, check that they are healthy.

Choose a fish with bright, clear eyes and shiny skin. It should not be slow-moving, or have split or damaged **fins**. If the fish looks like this, it may be unwell.

A healthy fish should be active with upright fins.

Setting up your tank

Your fish needs a tank to live in. A tank
that measures 90 x 38 x 30 cm will have
room for five to eight small fish.

Place your tank out of bright
sunlight and draughts.

You need to fill the tank with water but you must mix tap water with special liquids first. Put **gravel** and stones in the bottom to make it interesting for your fish.

Ask an adult to help you fix a **water filter** to the tank. It will keep the water clean. You will also need an **air pump** to control the amount of **oxygen** in the water.

Putting in plants

It is a good idea to put some water plants into your tank. You can dig small holes in the **gravel** and push the plants in.

There are lots of different types of water plants to choose from. These are waterweed, anubias nana and amazon compacta.

Plants are useful because they make **oxygen** for your fish to breathe. Your fish will also like to swim and hide among their leaves.

Plants look best in groups, with the taller ones at the back.

Welcome home

You can carry your fish home in a plastic bag. Then you should float the bag of fish in your tank for 20 minutes.

When you need to move your fish, do not touch them with your hands. Use a net or jug.

This makes sure that the **temperature** of the water in the bag is the same as in the tank. Then let your fish out of the bag.

If you tip your fish straight into the tank, the different water temperatures may cause stress and make your goldfish ill.

Feeding time

You can buy special goldfish food from a pet shop. You can also give your fish some chopped lettuce or spinach leaves.

Special fish flakes give your fish all the goodness they need.

Feed your fish once a day. Take care
not to give your fish too much food.
It can turn bad and **poison** the water.

Watch your fish swim to the
surface to gobble up their food.

Cleaning the tank

It is important to look after your tank to keep your fish healthy. Every day, check that the water is clean and your fish are swimming about.

Your goldfish will quickly become ill in a dirty tank.

Every two weeks, change part of the water in the tank. Clean the tank thoroughly. Cut back any plants that have grown too tall or bushy.

Clean any green **slime** off the inside of the glass with a scraper.

Growing up

Goldfish get bigger as they grow into adults. Watch how big your fish grow and make sure that your tank does not get overcrowded.

Fish that are about 7 cm long are the best size for your tank.

If your goldfish grow longer than 12 cm, they should live in an outside pond. In a pond, goldfish can grow very big.

If you have a garden, you might be able to make your own pond.

Healthy goldfish

Goldfish are very healthy pets if you care for them properly. If you think your goldfish looks ill, call your vet.

The vet will be able to tell you what is wrong with your goldfish.

If your fish seems to be moving slowly, it may not be well. Drooping **fins** or white spots on its skin are also signs of illness.

If a fish is ill, it is best to move it into a separate tank until it is better.

Old age

If you look after your goldfish well, they can live for many years. They do not need any special care as they get older.

A common goldfish can live for up to 25 years!

It can be very upsetting when a pet dies. Try not to be too sad. Just remember all the happy times that you shared.

Caring for your fish will help you learn how to treat animals properly.

Useful tips

- Wash your hands before and after you clean out the tank or feed your fish.

- Never tap the glass of the tank. This will annoy or shock your fish.

- Always keep the tank covered and out of reach of cats and other pets.

- Leave your fish to settle in for two weeks before you add any more.

- When you are cleaning out the tank, put your fish in some of the old water in a bucket.

- Never keep your fish in a goldfish bowl. There will not be enough **oxygen** for them to breathe.

Fact file

- Goldfish were first kept as pets by Chinese people over 4500 years ago.

- The oldest goldfish was thought to be over 50 years old when it died. It lived in China.

- Some common goldfish can grow 40 cm long.

- Not all goldfish are gold-coloured. Some are black, white, or even blue.

- A female goldfish lays 1000–3000 eggs at a time.

- Many 'fancy' types of goldfish have been bred, with features such as trailing fins or upturned eyes.

Glossary

air pump machine fixed to a fish tank to put oxygen into the water for your fish to breathe

fins flaps of skin that grow from a fish's sides and back

gills part of a fish's body that takes oxygen from the water so the fish can breathe

gravel tiny stones

hatch when baby fish come out of their eggs

oxygen gas that animals need to breathe to stay alive

poison something that causes illness or death

slime tiny plants that form a thin, green film on the tank

temperature how hot or cold something is

water filter machine fixed to the side of the fish tank to keep the water clean

More information

Books to read

A First Look at Animals: Pets, Claire Watts (Two-Can, 2000)

How to Look After Your Pet: Fish, Mark Evans (Dorling Kindersley, 1993)

The Official RSPCA Pet Guide: Care for your Goldfish (HarperCollins, 1991)

Websites

www.rspca.org.uk
   The website of The Royal Society for the Prevention of Cruelty to Animals in Britain.

www.pethealthcare.co.uk
   Information about keeping and caring for first pets.

www.petnet.com.au
   Information about being a good pet owner.

Index

Titles in the *A Pet's Life* series include:

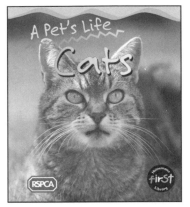

Hardback   0 431 17762 7

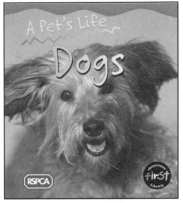

Hardback   0 431 17764 3

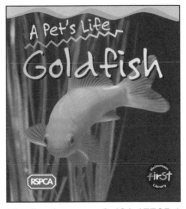

Hardback   0 431 17765 1

Hardback   0 431 17761 9

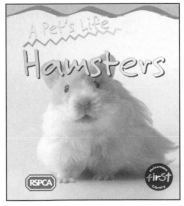

Hardback   0 431 17763 5

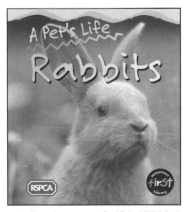

Hardback   0 431 17760 0

Find out about the other titles in this series on our website www.heinemann.co.uk/library